GARFIELD'S Book of Jokes and Riddles

Created by Jim Davis
Written by Mark Acey and Scott Nickel
Designed by Kenny Goetzinger
Illustrated by Paws, Inc.

Copyright © 1997 by PAWS. Published by Troll Communications L.L.C. All rights reserved.
Printed in the United States of America. ISBN 0-8167-4290-1
10 9 8 7 6 5 4 3 2 1

Why did Garfield swat the fly?
It was bugging him.

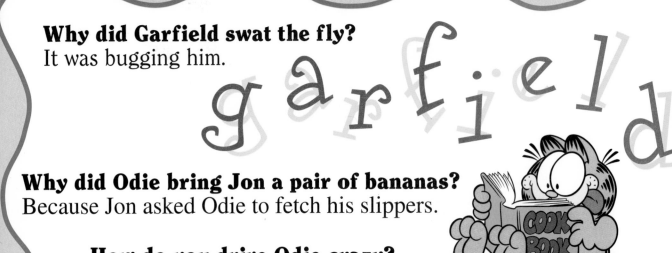

Why did Odie bring Jon a pair of bananas?
Because Jon asked Odie to fetch his slippers.

How do you drive Odie crazy?
Put him in a round room and tell
him to go stand in the corner.

**What's Garfield's
favorite kind of book?**
A cookbook.

What's just as big as Garfield but doesn't weigh a single pound?
Garfield's shadow.

giggles

If Garfield were a vegetable, what kind would he be?
A couch potato.

Why did Garfield cross the road?
To get to the pizza parlor
on the other side.

**What do you call Odie
after Garfield soaks
him with water?**
A soggy doggy.

How does Garfield feel about winter?
It leaves him cold.

What did Garfield say after he pushed Odie off the table?
"Doggone."

SCHOOL

Why did the spider like computers?
Because he had his own Web site.

**What would you call a
surprise test about Odie?**
A *pup* quiz.

**Why did the firefly
skip a grade?**
He was very bright.

DAZE

What bait should you use to catch a school of fish?
Bookworms.

How do cows count?
They use *cow*culators.

Why does Garfield like computers?
Because he can play with the mouse, but he doesn't have to eat it.

What is a witch's favorite subject?
Spell-ing.

What are Garfield's three favorite countries?
Turkey, Chile, and Greece.

What would you have if you crossed Nermal with a glove?
The world's cutest mitten.

What do you call a kitten that does somersaults in the air?
An acro-cat.

What do anteaters like on their pizzas?
Ant-chovies.

Where do polar bears keep their money?
In snowbanks.

What's the difference between a dog and a flea?
A dog can have fleas, but a flea can't have dogs.

Did you hear the one about...?

Did you hear the one about the Liberty Bell?
It cracks me up.

Did you hear the one about the werewolf?
It's a howler.

Did you hear the one about the spaceship?
It's out of this world.

Did you hear the one about the red pepper?
It's hot stuff.

Did you hear the one about the teacher?
It's in a class by itself.

Nutty

Knock, knock.
Who's there?
Kareem.
Kareem who?
Kareem-filled cupcakes
are Garfield's favorite.

Knock, knock.
Who's there?
Bea.
Bea who?
Bea my valentine?

Knock, knock.
Who's there?
Anita.
Anita who?
Anita more food – here comes Garfield.

Knock, knock.
Who's there?
Bach.
Bach who?
Bach like a dog.

GARFI

Knock, knock.
Who's there?
Jackie-Anne.
Jackie-Anne who?
Jackie-Anne Jilly
went up the hilly.

Knock-Knocks

Knock, knock.
Who's there?
José.
José who?
José can you see
by the dawn's
early light?

Knock, knock.
Who's there?
Scott.
Scott who?
Scott a million
of these jokes.

Knock, knock.
Who's there?
Leah.
Leah who?
Leah me alone.

**Who's orange and furry
and doesn't like Toto?**
The Wizard Of Paws.

**What would you get if you
crossed Garfield with
Quasimodo?**
The Munchcat of Notre Dame.

**Who lives in Sherwood Forest
and is really messy?**
Slobbin Hood.

**Knock, knock.
Who's there?
Aladdin.
Aladdin who?
Aladdin my class has a
girlfriend named Jeannie.**

**What's Garfield's
favorite fairy tale?**
Beauty and the Feast.

Tricky Tongue Twisters

Can you say these three times fast?

Shaq sadly shot three free throws

Roy writes wacky radical wild riddles

Fleas frazzle fat flabby feline

Crazy clown's crown

Sheep shorn short sleep soundly

Jon's sweaty socks make Jon's suede shoes smell

SCARED

How did Garfield make the skeleton laugh?
He tickled his funny bone.

What did the sad ghost say to Garfield?
Boo-hoo.

What do monsters like to snack on?
Ghoul Scout cookies.

What kind of music do mummies like?
Wrap music.

What do spooks eat for dinner?
Ghost beef.

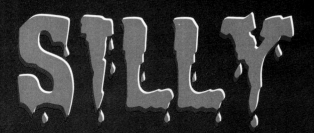

SILLY

What's the tallest building in Transylvania?
The Vampire State building.

Where do vampires keep their money?
In a blood bank.

What did the mad doctor get when he crossed a skunk with his monster?
Stinkinstein.

What would you get if you crossed Dracula with Odie?
A vampire who slobbers on your neck.

SPORT SHORTS

Where do trains race?
At track meets.

What's Garfield's favorite sport?
Mice hockey.

Why did Garfield wear sneakers?
So he could sneak up on Odie.

Why isn't Odie good at basketball?
Because he can drool, but he can't dribble.

**What two letters describe
a slippery street?**
IC

What two letters are the opposite of difficult?
EZ

What two letters describe Odie's breath?
PU

What two letters describe Odie's head?
MT

**What two letters
does Garfield most
like to watch?**
TV

Food Funnies

**What kind of cake
do mice like?**
Cheesecake.

What are the two things Garfield can never eat for breakfast?
Lunch and dinner.

**What does Garfield eat
when he's grouchy?**
Crab meat.

**On what day does Garfield
cook hamburgers?**
Fry-day.

**Knock, knock.
Who's there?
Bacon.
Bacon who?
Bacon cookies just for you.**

**What do you get when a
dinosaur walks through a
vegetable garden?**
Squash.

FEED
the
COOK

If Garfield had ten doughnuts in one paw and nine doughnuts in the other, what would he have?
Big paws.

What is Garfield's least favorite cake?
A cake of soap.

What do frogs drink?
Croak-a-cola.

What does a shark eat with peanut butter?
Jellyfish.

What happens to Garfield when he eats a lemon?
He becomes a sourpuss.

WHAT CAN IT BE?
Can You Figure Out These Brain Teasers?

1. What kind of coat is easy to put on, but hard to take off?

2. What has a neck but no head?

3. What has three feet but can't walk?

4. What has a face and hands but no feet?

5. What has teeth but can't bite?

6. What always eats, but is never full?

7. What is full of holes but holds water?

8. What gets wet as it dries?

9. What has two legs but can't walk?

10. What can Garfield take but not give back?

ANSWERS

1. A coat of paint. 2. A bottle. 3. A yard. 4. A clock. 5. A comb.
6. Garfield! 7. A sponge. 8. A towel. 9. A pair of pants. 10. A nap.

**What would you get if you
crossed a bear with a skunk?**
Winnie the Pew.

**What's nice, flies through
walls, and eats tin cans?**
Casper the Friendly Goat.

Where does Superman shop for food?
At the supermarket, of course.

**What would you get if you crossed a
smarter-than-average bear with a rabbit?**
Yogi Hare.

**Who has
webbed feet
and fights crime?**
Duck Tracy.

Why did the woman go to the hardware store?
She wanted long nails.

What do you call a sleeping dinosaur?
A Tyranno-snore-us Rex.

JEST FOR LAUGHS

Why did Jon take a broom to the dance?
So he could sweep the girls off their feet.

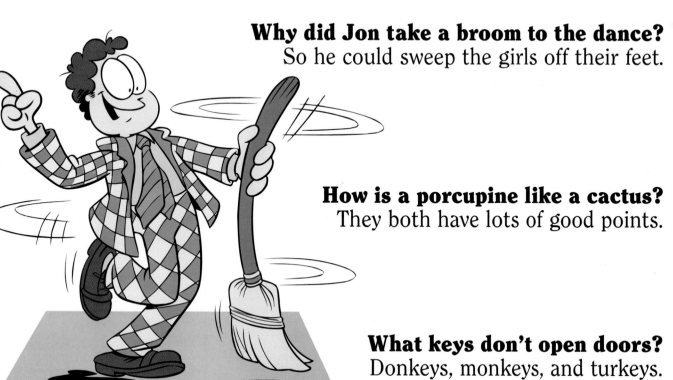

How is a porcupine like a cactus?
They both have lots of good points.

What keys don't open doors?
Donkeys, monkeys, and turkeys.

Knock, knock.
Who's there?
Juan.
Juan who?
Juan plus Juan equals two.

Knock, knock.
Who's there?
Roach.
Roach who?
Roach you a letter but you didn't answer.

MORE
Nutty
Knock-
Knocks

Knock, knock.
Who's there?
Candy.
Candy who?
Candy dog play with de bone?

Knock, knock.
Who's there?
Freddy.
Freddy who?
Freddy or not,
here I come.

Knock, knock.
Who's there?
Drew.
Drew who?
Drew a picture of
Garfield and Odie.

Knock, knock.
Who's there?
Feline.
Feline who?
Feline blue, because
you won't let me in.

Knock, knock.
Who's there?
Carrie.
Carrie who?
Carrie Garfield? He's way too heavy.

Knock, knock.
Who's there?
Ben.
Ben who?
Ben there.
Done that.

**What would you get if you crossed
a dinosaur with a pig?**
Jurassic pork.

What do you call a croaking pig?
Kermit the Hog.

**What's 100 feet tall, orange,
and eats its way through Japan?**
Garzilla.

What would you get if you crossed Odie with a deer?
Dumbi.